# KERRY LORD

## HOW TO CROCHET ANIMALS
# FARM
### 25 MINI MENAGERIE PATTERNS

#edsanimals
@toft_uk

PAVILION

# CONTENTS

Introduction                                    4
How to Use This Book                            6
TOFT                                            7

**BASICS**
Essential Tools                                 8
Extra Tools                                     9
Yarn                                           10
Tension                                        11
Holding Your Hook                              12
Holding Your Yarn                              13
Learning to Crochet                            14
Counting Your Stitches                         17
Reading a Pattern and Abbreviations            18

## PROJECTS

| | |
|---|---|
| Pig | 20 |
| Hare | 28 |
| Sheep | 30 |
| Alpaca | 34 |
| Hedgehog | 36 |
| Goose | 40 |
| Frog | 44 |
| Chick | 48 |
| Donkey | 52 |
| Goat | 58 |
| Pony | 60 |
| Badger | 62 |
| Mole | 64 |
| Dorset Down Sheep | 68 |
| Fox | 70 |
| Robin | 72 |
| Friesian Cow | 76 |
| Pheasant | 78 |
| Bat | 80 |
| Swaledale Sheep | 84 |
| Snail | 88 |
| Squirrel | 94 |
| Border Collie | 96 |
| Shire Horse | 98 |
| Highland Cow | 102 |

| | |
|---|---|
| Others in the Series | 104 |
| Be Social | 106 |
| Animal Index | 108 |
| Technique Index | 109 |
| Thanks | 110 |
| About the Author | 111 |

# INTRODUCTION

I hope this book will be a brilliant introduction to crochet for anyone picking up a hook for the first time, but also give a lot of enjoyment to anyone already familiar with the double crochet stitch. I believe learning to crochet is something that should be done with the clear motivation of a pattern to master and the resulting feeling of accomplishment when that project is complete.  These quick and easy crochet animals are a great way to start to learn a range of basic and more advanced crochet techniques, and the variety of projects and progression of difficulty across the twenty-five patterns should keep even a seasoned maker entertained and challenged.

I learned to crochet from a video that taught me the British double crochet stitch (US single crochet). Like with anything new, to begin with holding a hook and yarn felt awkward and unfamiliar, but even after just a few hours of perseverance I found my way of holding the hook and working the stitches, and discovered how much fun you could have with just one simple technique. This book is a gathering together of all of my experience learning to crochet and teaching people to crochet over the last eight years. I am completely humbled by the idea that through the Edward's Menagerie pattern series I have been able to teach not only thousands of people face to face to crochet through workshops and events, but have also inspired millions of people worldwide with all my books and TOFT video tutorials. Learning to crochet completely changed my life, and I hope I can share out the happiness mastering this hobby has brought me as far and wide as possible.

TOFT is a company I started fourteen years ago with no idea what it would grow to become. Our vision is to enrich the lives of as many people as possible with our shared love of craft, and our mission is to be as creative and original as possible making products to inspire that in others. We specialise in luxury natural yarns and quality long-lasting tools that come together in your hands to give you pleasure as you savour the feeling of making the stitches, and spread happiness with the results of your time.

Within these pages you'll find the most popular farm animals alongside some British wildlife that a farmer would very likely cross paths with on her day in the fields. I hope you enjoy the variety of domesticated and wild animals in this book and can make your own fantasy farms with all your favourite breeds. This book of mini patterns forms part of a series also including WILD, OCEAN and PETS, so once you've enjoyed crocheting a sheep or chick a few times you might want to turn your hands to a tiger or maybe a goldfish or two.

For me crochet is a bit of a counterpoint to the busy rhythm and routine of my life, it allows me to feel creative after a long day that might have otherwise felt very mundane, and these mini animals make brilliant gifts for friends and family without being too much of a materials or time investment. Although it may be slower when you are starting out, once you've got a couple under your belt these mini patterns are the perfect size to make in an evening. So, when you've got a craft itch to scratch, grab a hook, a handful of your favourite yarn and carve out a few hours to relax. Enjoy the mindfulness of the double crochet stitch and the focus and rewards it brings.

*Kerry Lord*

# HOW TO USE THIS BOOK

The projects in this book are arranged in order of difficulty, with their corresponding techniques and progressive skills detailed when they are introduced.

If you are learning to crochet, then start at the beginning and turn each page, reading all the tips and trying a few of the exercises to get you used to holding your hook and yarn before you dive into working your first project.

If you are already a confident crocheter, then start with whatever takes your fancy and dip in and out of the projects. If you hit an abbreviation or instruction you are unsure of and would like to refresh your understanding then use the technique index on page 109 to find the full step-by-step breakdown.

All the standard stuffing and sewing up details can be found on page 23. Follow these guidelines unless the pattern says different. Unless otherwise stated in the pattern, once you have worked the last round of the pattern gather the stitches once fastening off a part using the technique detailed on page 24.

I have used British English crochet terms throughout. 'Double crochet' (dc) is the same as the American English 'single crochet' (sc). For clarification of which stitch this refers to please see the basic instruction for the dc stitch on page 15.

# TOFT

All the projects in this book are created using TOFT pure wool double knitting yarn on a 3mm aluminum hook with a pure wool stuffing. I have had the pleasure of selecting, designing and manufacturing luxury yarns for the past fourteen years as the founder of the TOFT brand, and Edward's Menagerie has been inspired by this range of yarns. TOFT yarns are luxury, quality, natural fibres manufactured to my distinctive specifications here in the UK. When crocheted in TOFT yarns, the projects in this book are supple and soft but with a closed fabric to hide the stuffing inside.

Using natural fibres is not only better for the environment, but also ensures a beautiful finish, assures you that these animals will only get better over time and guarantees each stitch is a pleasure to make.

TOFT is here to help if you are new to crochet and not sure where to begin, and the brand is based in a real place called Toft in Warwickshire, England. In addition to our yarns, TOFT now designs and manufactures a whole range of tools and accessories to accompany the Edward's Menagerie crochet range. Video help is on-hand if you are struggling at any point with the techniques in this book. All materials, kits and videos for these projects are available at **www.toftuk.com**.

# ESSENTIAL TOOLS

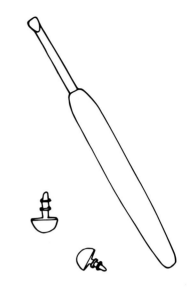

### HOOK
Choose the right sized hook to match your yarn and create the correct tension (see page 11). If you're buying a hook for the first time, get a good quality one with a comfortable handle as it also doubles as the perfect tool for teasing the toy stuffing inside small parts.

### STITCH MARKER
Marking the start or end of your rounds when working this style of crochet is essential. I recommend using a piece of contrast yarn, approximately 15cm long, positioned in the last stitch of Round 2. As you return back around to your marker, pull it forwards or backwards through or between your stitches to mark the end of the round you have just finished to help you keep track of where you are in the pattern. The marker will weave up the fabric with you, and you can simply pull it free to remove it at the end. Should you ever need to abandon your crochet halfway through a round of instruction, or if you simply lose you place when counting, you will be able to return to your marker and thus never have to do a total restart.

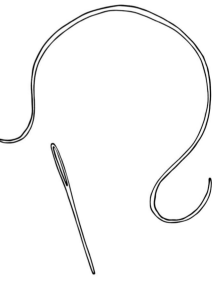

### SCISSORS
Sharp scissors or snips are good for cutting the ends once you've finished sewing up.

### STUFFING
You can use a natural or man-made stuffing material inside your animals. Using polyester stuffing will make them easier to wash by hand or in a cool cycle in the machine.

### SEWING NEEDLE
Ensure your sewing needle has a big enough eye to make it easy to thread your chosen yarn.

### CONTRAST YARN OR SAFETY EYES
I have used black yarn to sew on all of the animals' eyes and noses. Although safety eyes could be added before sewing up, please be aware these should not be used on a toy for a child under five years of age.

# EXTRA TOOLS

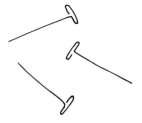

### ROW COUNTER

Use a row counter if following a pattern is a new discipline for you. It may make it easier to keep a track of your pattern if you do not wish to mark your place in the book.

### PROJECT BAG

Although not essential, a project bag can be very handy to keep your latest make safe and in order, especially if you are transporting your crochet with you on a commute or to make the most of your lunch break.

### PINS FOR SEWING UP

If you are new to making 3D crochet then pins might help you position all the parts before sewing them together. While not essential, they can come in handy if you know that sewing the eyes and ears onto the faces poses a challenge for your perfectionism.

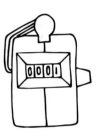

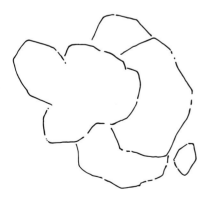

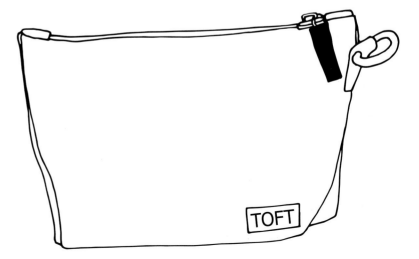

# YARN

I was inspired to learn to crochet and make these patterns by TOFT yarn, and all of the animals in this book have been created in TOFT's pure wool double knitting (DK) yarn using a 3mm hook. Each animal takes around 18–30g of TOFT yarn and the finished height is 10cm. TOFT DK pure wool yarn comes in a spectrum of twelve natural colours (opposite) and twelve brights. From the top, they are Ruby, Orange, Yellow, Lime, Green, Teal, Turquoise, Blue, Sapphire, Amethyst, Magenta and Pink.

The quantity of yarn needed in the projects is based on using TOFT yarns. If using other brands of yarn, the quantities may vary significantly, depending on the fibre composition and spinning specifications of the yarn. Parts that use loop stitch or upon which you work chain loops will take considerably more yarn that's others – for example, don't skimp when starting the alpaca!

# TENSION

SILVER

CREAM

OATMEAL

SHALE

STONE

STEEL

If you are seeing holes in your fabric when working the patterns, swap your hook size down half a millimeter. Likewise, if your work is too solid and you are finding the stitches hard to work, then swap up half a millimetre. The legs on this page are made using TOFT double knitting yarn and a 3mm hook. The standard tension of TOFT DK yarn on a 3mm hook is 3 x 3cm = 6 sts x 7 rnds.

CHARCOAL

CAMEL

COCOA

MUSHROOM

CHESTNUT

FUDGE

# HOLDING YOUR HOOK

There are two principal ways of holding your crochet hook, one similar to holding a knife and the other to holding a pencil. If you are totally new to crochet, I would recommend the knife hold as easier to get comfortable with and maintain control and a good tension, but if you already use the pencil hold successfully then do not alter it. Even within these two holds there are lots of subtle variants on how to hold your hook and there is no wrong or right way. Do what is most comfortable for you.

**Knife hold**

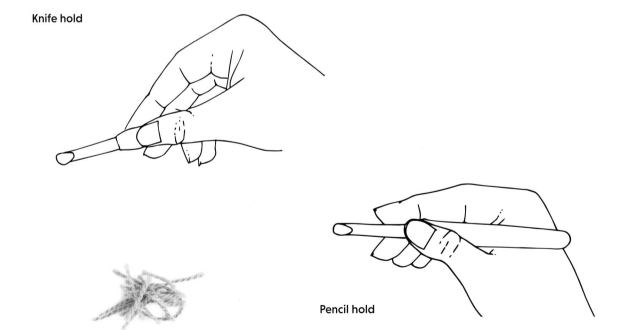

**Pencil hold**

# HOLDING YOUR YARN

Every crocheter I meet holds their yarn in a slightly different way, so use these illustrations as a rough guide and then experiment with what's most comfortable for you. Only adjust your hand position if you think the way you hold the yarn is causing a problem: loose stitches can be caused by not putting tension onto the yarn coming off the ball by wrapping around your finger, but the opposite problem of the yarn not moving freely can often be worse and you will feel like you are fighting the stitches and creating a very tight tension.

If you are left-handed, there are no special changes you need to make as none of the patterns in this book refers to left and right.

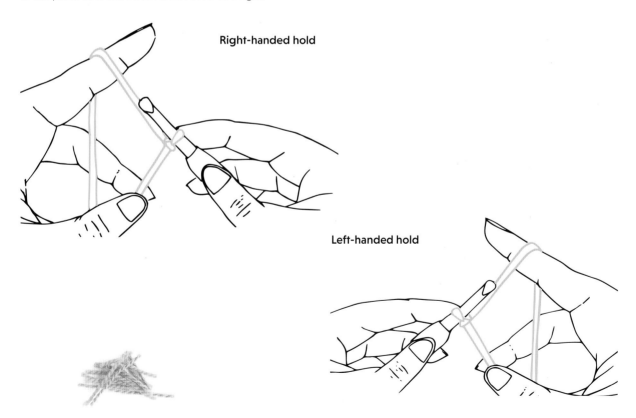

**Right-handed hold**

**Left-handed hold**

# LEARNING TO CROCHET

Practise your hook and hand positions from the previous pages by working a long chain length. It will help you get used to coordinating both hands and find what works best for you. If you are comfortable working the stitches and achieving the correct tension, there is no wrong or right.

## SLIP KNOT

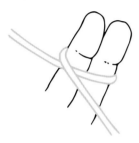

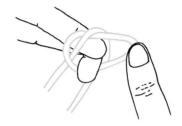

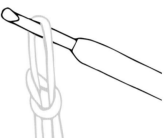

1 Wrap the yarn around your fingers.

2 Pull the tail end of the yarn through the wrap to make a loop.

3 Place your hook through the loop and tighten, ensuring that it is the tail end of the yarn (not the ball end) that controls the opening and closing of the knot.

## CHAIN (CH)

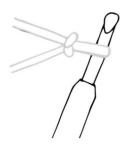

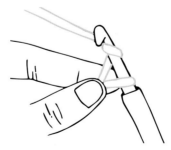

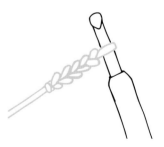

1 Make a slip knot.

2 Wrap the yarn over the hook (yarn over) and pull it through the loop on the hook.

3 Repeat until desired length.

## DOUBLE CROCHET STITCH (DC)

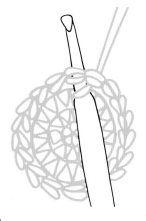 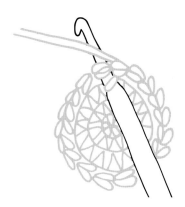 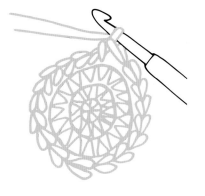

**1** Insert the hook through the stitch under both loops of the 'V' unless otherwise stated.

**2** Yarn over, rotate hook head, and pull through the stitch (two loops on hook).

**3** Yarn over again and pull through both loops on the hook to end with one loop on the hook (one double crochet stitch made).

## DC6 INTO RING (MAGIC CIRCLE)

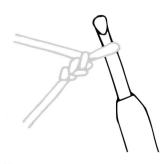 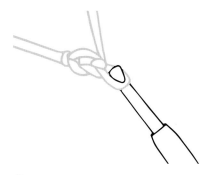 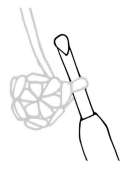

**1** Make a slip knot and chain two stitches.

**2** Insert the hook into the first chain stitch made and work a double crochet six times into this same stitch.

**3** Pull tightly on the tail of the yarn to close the centre of the ring and form a neat circle.

## DECREASING (DC2TOG)

 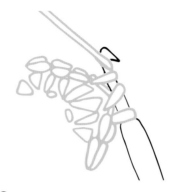 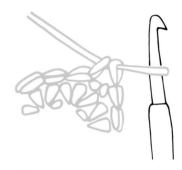

1  Insert the hook under the front loop only of the next stitch (two loops on hook).

2  In the same motion insert the hook through the front loop only of the following stitch (three loops on hook).

3  Yarn over and pull through the first two loops on the hook, then yarn over and pull through both remaining loops to complete the double crochet decrease.

## FASTENING OFF

Once you have finished a piece, you'll need to fasten off the yarn to secure it so the stitch does not unravel.

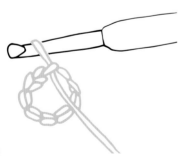 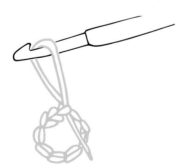 

1  When finishing the last stitch of any round simply cut the yarn leaving 8–10cm for sewing up.

2  Pull your hook upwards away from your work until the end goes through the loop on hook.

3  Pull to tighten.

# COUNTING YOUR STITCHES

An essential skill to keep yourself on track and able to follow the pattern accurately is knowing how to count the number of stitches you have in a round. While learning, count your stitches in a round after each line of pattern that involves increasing or decreasing. The number in brackets at the end of a line of pattern indicates the number of stitches you should have once it is completed. If you complete a round and this number is wrong, then pull back your work to the beginning of the round and redo it until you have the correct number of stitches before you progress – this is much easier with a stitch marker (see page 8).

### COUNTING A CHAIN
When you crochet a chain and then work back down it you will often miss the stitch closest to you hook in order to turn. For example you might chain 10 stitches in order to double crochet 9 stitches back down the chain.

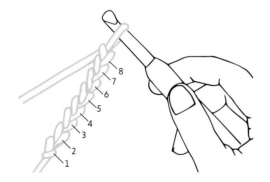

### COUNTING THE STITCHES IN A ROUND
The majority of the time your crochet piece will grow from a set number of stitches in a closed ring (usually six). The piece you are making grows because you are increasing the number of stitches by sometimes working two double crochet into the same stitch as instructed.

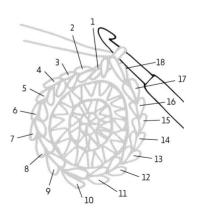

# READING A PATTERN AND ABBREVIATIONS

**RND: ROUND**
A round is a complete rotation in a spiral back to where you started. In this style of crochet you DO NOT slip stitch at the end of a round to make a circle, but instead continue directly on to the next round in a spiral.

**STS: STITCHES**
The number in brackets at the end of a line indicates the number of stitches in that round once it has been completed.

Begin by dc6 into ring

Rnd 1 (dc2 into next st) 6 times (12 sts)

Rnd 2 (dc1, dc2 into next st) 6 times (18)

Rnd 3 (dc2, dc2 into next st) 6 times (24)

Rnd 4 (dc3, dc2 into next st) 6 times (30)

Rnd 5 (dc4, dc2 into next st) 6 times (36)

Rnd 6 (dc5, dc2 into next st) 6 times (42)

Rnd 7 (dc6, dc2 into next st) 6 times (48)

Rnds 8–10 dc (3 rnds)

**6 TIMES**
Repeat what comes directly before this instruction within the brackets the number of times stated.

**DC: DOUBLE CROCHET**
Dc5 means to double crochet one stitch into each of the next five stitches.

**3 RNDS**
Work one double crochet stitch into every stitch in the round for three full rounds.

**Additional abbreviations**
ch: chain
dc2tog: double crochet two stitches together (to turn two stitches into one and decrease a round count by one stitch)
sl st: slip stitch

# BASICS OF
# SPIRAL CROCHET

When working the style of crochet used in this book to create a solid fabric and 3D shapes, you generally start from a closed ring and work the double crochet stitch in one direction in a non-stop spiral. The pattern on page 18 forms a pretty standard increase for this style of crochet by adding six stitches evenly into every round. The piece becomes 3D once you stop adding six stitches into a round.

### RIGHT SIDE (RS) AND WRONG SIDE (WS)

If you are new to this style of crochet, you do need to be aware that there is a right side (RS) and wrong side (WS) to the fabric; the wrong side forms the inside of the shape. If you are right-handed and crocheting with the RS facing outwards, you will be moving in an anti-clockwise direction around the edge of the circle of fabric (left-handed people will be moving clockwise). It is very easy to have learned to crochet holding your WS facing outwards (I did it myself); this will mean that your resulting piece is inside out when you come to stuff and finish it. With some parts this will not be a problem, as you can simply flip them before stuffing and sewing up. However, with the parts containing smaller rounds, such as tails, this will be impossible, so it is best to adjust your hold to ensure you are crocheting into the RS of the fabric with this on the outside of the 3D shape. On the RS of the fabric you will see the rounds horizontally on the piece. On the WS you can see vertical furrows spiralling up the piece.

Follow the pattern opposite to practise your double crochet stitches before starting your first animal. Once you feel more familiar with the stitch on this bigger piece, it will be easier to work the smaller rounds required in many of the minis.

# PIG

## BODY
Begin by dc6 into ring
**Rnd 1** (dc2 into next st) 6 times (12 sts)
**Rnd 2** (dc1, dc2 into next st) 6 times (18)
**Rnd 3** (dc2, dc2 into next st) 6 times (24)
**Rnds 4–8** dc (5 rnds)
**Rnd 9** dc9 , (dc2tog) 3 times, dc9 (21)
**Rnd 10** (dc5, dc2tog) 3 times (18)
**Rnds 11–13** dc (3 rnds)
**Rnd 14** (dc4, dc2tog) 3 times (15)
**Rnd 15** (dc3, dc2tog) 3 times (12)
**Rnd 16** (dc2tog) 6 times (6)

## HEAD
Begin by dc6 into ring
**Rnd 1** (dc2 into next st) 6 times (12)
**Rnd 2** (dc1, dc2 into next st) 6 times (18)
**Rnd 3** (dc2, dc2 into next st) 6 times (24)
**Rnds 4–6** dc (3 rnds)
**Rnd 7** (dc1, dc2tog) 6 times, dc6 (18)
**Rnd 8** (dc1, dc2tog) twice, dc12 (16)
**Rnd 9** (dc2, dc2tog) 4 times (12)
**Rnds 10–12** dc (3 rnds)
**Rnd 13** (dc2, dc2tog) 3 times (9)

## LEGS (make four)
Begin by dc6 into ring
**Rnd 1** (dc2 into next st) 6 times (12)
**Rnds 2–3** dc (2 rnds)
**Rnd 4** (dc1, dc2tog) 4 times (8)
**Rnds 5–12** dc (8 rnds)
Stuff end and sew flat across top to close.

## EARS (make two)
Begin by dc6 into ring
**Rnd 1** (dc2 into next st) 6 times (12)
**Rnd 2** (dc1, dc2 into next st) 6 times (18)
**Rnd 3** (dc2, dc2 into next st) 6 times (24)
Fold in half RS out and dc6 through both edges
   to create point
Sew into position on head.

## TAIL
Sl st into tail position and work ch4 SLIP STITCH CHAIN (see
   page 39) as follows:
dc4 into first ch, (dc3 into next ch) twice

Finish by sewing eyes and nostrils into place
   with Black yarn.

A perfect place to start with a light-coloured
yarn and your first 3D shapes

## ORDER OF SEWING

1. Sew the head onto the body with two stitches between the top of the body and under the head (all heads start from the back and work forwards). Once lined up with the tummy, oversew around these stitches in a small circle between the two parts to secure.
2. Sew the front legs to the top of the body.
3. Sew the back legs to the bottom of the body in the position shown on page 24.
4. Sew on the ears, remembering that often they should be positioned further back on the head rather than the top.
5. Add the eyes and nose or nostrils if specified.
6. Sew the tail into position (if required) and complete with any chain surface detail if specified.

## STUFFING (USING BACK OF HOOK)

When using TOFT pure wool your fabric is forgiving and supple and this combines really well with light-handed stuffing to create animals that feel soft to the touch rather than dense or stiff. You want to show off the shaping within the piece but not overstuff it until that is lost and the stuffing shows through the stitches. Only stuff the feet of the legs.

## GATHERING STITCHES

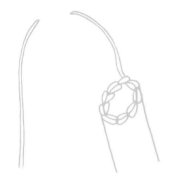

1   Fasten off the last stitch of the round.

2   Thread the end of the yarn onto a sewing needle and sew a running stitch through all the remaining stitches of the round.

3   Pull tightly to gather and close the stitches, then fasten off into the fabric around a stitch.

## OVERSEWING A LEG

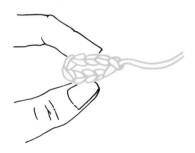

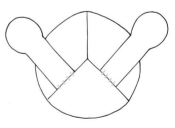

Back leg position

1   Flatten the top of the leg between finger and thumb, aligning the stitches neatly.

2   Sew through pairs of stitches along the edge to close the top of the leg flat.

3   Oversew the leg into position.

## ADDING THE TAIL

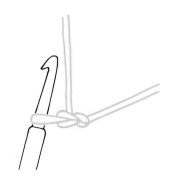
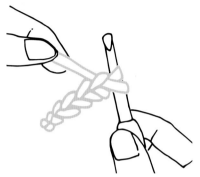
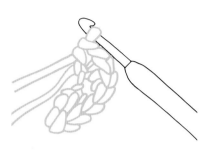

1 Insert the hook through the fabric at the desired position, yarn over and pull through the fabric.

2 Chain the number of stitches stated in the pattern.

3 Working back down the chain dc2 into each ch st to create a spiral tail

### SEWING ON EYES/NOSTRILS
1. Sew through the piece into top position of first eye (or nostril).
2. Sew down around one stitch.
3. Move through inside of piece and repeat for second eye (or nostril).

If using safety eyes don't forget to add before gathering your stitches but after the stuffing. The character of your animal is dictated by the position of the ears, nose and most importantly the eyes. A face with larger eyes will look younger and more cute, ears sewn low down the sides of the head will look sleepy and adding a nose or two very simple nostrils can suddenly add the finishing touch.

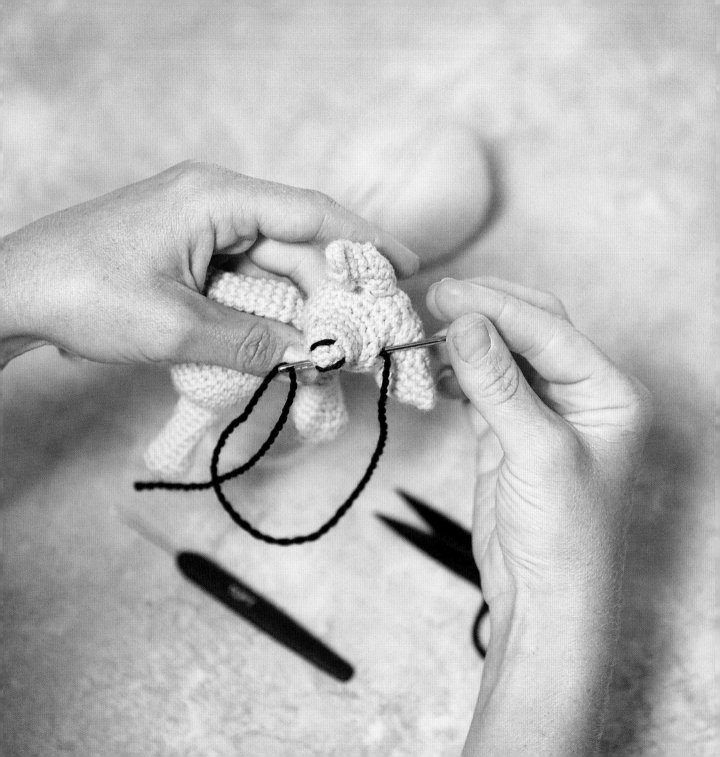

# HARE

## BODY
Begin by dc6 into ring
**Rnd 1** (dc2 into next st) 6 times (12 sts)
**Rnd 2** (dc1, dc2 into next st) 6 times (18)
**Rnd 3** (dc2, dc2 into next st) 6 times (24)
**Rnds 4–8** dc (5 rnds)
**Rnd 9** dc9, (dc2tog) 3 times, dc9 (21)
**Rnd 10** (dc5, dc2tog) 3 times (18)
**Rnds 11–13** dc (3 rnds)
**Rnd 14** (dc4, dc2tog) 3 times (15)
**Rnd 15** (dc3, dc2tog) 3 times (12)
**Rnd 16** (dc2tog) 6 times (6)

## HEAD
Begin by dc6 into ring
**Rnd 1** (dc2 into next st) 6 times (12)
**Rnd 2** (dc1, dc2 into next st) 6 times (18)
**Rnd 3** (dc2, dc2 into next st) 6 times (24)
**Rnds 4–6** dc (3 rnds)
**Rnd 7** (dc2, dc2tog) 6 times (18)
**Rnd 8** (dc1, dc2tog) 6 times (12)
**Rnd 9** dc
**Rnd 10** (dc2tog) 6 times (6)

## LEGS (make four)
Begin by dc6 into ring
**Rnd 1** (dc2 into next st) 6 times (12)
**Rnds 2–3** dc (2 rnds)
**Rnd 4** (dc1, dc2tog) 4 times (8)
**Rnds 5–12** dc (8 rnds)
Stuff end and sew flat across top to close.

## EARS (make two)
Begin by dc6 into ring
**Rnd 1** (dc1, dc2 into next st) 3 times (9)
**Rnds 2–10** dc (9 rnds)
Do not stuff.

## TAIL
Begin by dc6 into ring
**Rnd 1** dc
Sew into position.

Finish by sewing eyes into place with Black yarn.

# SHEEP

**BODY**
Begin by dc6 into ring
**Rnd 1** (dc2 into next st) 6 times (12 sts)
**Rnd 2** (dc1, dc2 into next st) 6 times (18)
**Rnd 3** (dc2, dc2 into next st) 6 times (24)
**Rnds 4–8** dc (5 rnds)
**Rnd 9** dc9, (dc2tog) 3 times, dc9 (21)
**Rnd 10** (dc5, dc2tog) 3 times (18)
**Rnds 11–13** dc (3 rnds)
**Rnd 14** (dc4, dc2tog) 3 times (15)
**Rnd 15** (dc3, dc2tog) 3 times (12)
**Rnd 16** (dc2tog) 6 times (6)

**HEAD**
Begin by dc6 into ring
**Rnd 1** (dc2 into next st) 6 times (12)
**Rnd 2** (dc1, dc2 into next st) 6 times (18)
**Rnd 3** (dc2, dc2 into next st) 6 times (24)
**Rnds 4–6** dc (3 rnds)
**Rnd 7** (dc2tog) 3 times, dc18 (21)
**Rnd 8** (dc5, dc2tog) 3 times (18)
**Rnd 9** dc
**Rnd 10** (dc4, dc2tog) 3 times (15)
**Rnd 11** (dc3, dc2tog) 3 times (12)
**Rnd 12** (dc2tog) 6 times (6)

**LEGS** (make four)
Begin by dc6 into ring
**Rnd 1** (dc2 into next st) 6 times (12)
**Rnds 2–3** dc (2 rnds)
**Rnd 4** (dc1, dc2tog) 4 times (8)
**Rnds 5–12** dc (8 rnds)
Stuff end and sew flat across top to close.

**EARS** (make two)
Begin by dc5 into ring
**Rnds 1–2** dc (2 rnds)
Do not stuff.

**TAIL**
Begin by dc5 into ring
**Rnds 1–8** dc (8 rnds)
Do not stuff.

**FLEECE**
Work ch5 CHAIN LOOPS (see page 33) all over the body,
leaving the bottom where the legs are attached plain to
ensure balance when sitting.

Finish by sewing eyes and nose into place with Black yarn.

Use a simple chain to create a totally
new texture to your animals with this curly-
looking fleece.

## CHAIN LOOPS

1 Insert the hook through the fabric at the desired position, yarn over and pull through the fabric.

2 Chain the number of stitches stated in the pattern.

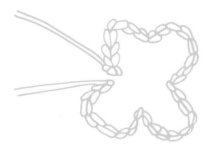

3 Attach the chain to the fabric with a slip stitch approximately two stitches or two rounds away from the start of the chain. Repeat until the required area is covered.

The fleece loops will look spread out with wide gaps when you start, but persevere with the two stitch spacing. Build them too densely and your project could become very stiff and heavy.

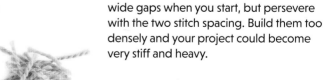

# ALPACA

## BODY
Begin by dc6 into ring
**Rnd 1** (dc2 into next st) 6 times (12 sts)
**Rnd 2** (dc1, dc2 into next st) 6 times (18)
**Rnd 3** (dc2, dc2 into next st) 6 times (24)
**Rnds 4–8** dc (5 rnds)
**Rnd 9** dc9, (dc2tog) 3 times, dc9 (21)
**Rnd 10** (dc5, dc2tog) 3 times (18)
**Rnds 11–13** dc (3 rnds)
**Rnd 14** (dc4, dc2tog) 3 times (15)
**Rnds 15–17** dc (3 rnds)
**Rnd 18** (dc3, dc2tog) 3 times (12)
**Rnd 19** (dc2tog) 6 times (6)

## HEAD
Begin by dc6 into ring
**Rnd 1** (dc2 into next st) 6 times (12)
**Rnd 2** (dc1, dc2 into next st) 6 times (18)
**Rnd 3** (dc2, dc2 into next st) 6 times (24)
**Rnds 4–6** dc (3 rnds)
**Rnd 7** (dc2tog) 3 times, dc18 (21)
**Rnd 8** (dc5, dc2tog) 3 times (18)
**Rnd 9** dc
**Rnd 10** (dc4, dc2tog) 3 times (15)
**Rnd 11** (dc3, dc2tog) 3 times (12)
**Rnd 12** dc
**Rnd 13** (dc2tog) 6 times (6)

## LEGS (make four)
Begin by dc6 into ring
**Round 1** (dc2 into next st) 6 times (12 sts)
**Rnds 2–3** dc (2 rnds)
**Rnd 4** (dc1, dc2tog) 4 times (8)
**Rnds 5–12** dc (8 rnds)
Stuff end and sew flat across top to close.

## EARS (make two)
Begin by dc5 into ring
**Rnds 1–2** dc (2 rnds)
Do not stuff.

## TAIL
Begin by dc6 into ring
**Rnds 1–2** dc (2 rnds)
**Rnd 3** (dc2tog) 3 times (3)

## FLEECE
Work ch5 CHAIN LOOPS (see page 33) all over the body
   and head, leaving the nose and the bottom where the
   legs are attached plain to ensure balance when sitting.

Finish by sewing eyes into place with Black yarn.

# HEDGEHOG

## BODY

Working in Fudge
Begin by dc6 into ring
**Rnd 1** (dc2 into next st) 6 times (12 sts)
**Rnd 2** (dc1, dc2 into next st) 6 times (18)
**Rnd 3** (dc2, dc2 into next st) 6 times (24)
**Rnds 4–8** dc (5 rnds)
**Rnd 9** dc9, (dc2tog) 3 times, dc9 (21)
**Rnd 10** (dc5, dc2tog) 3 times (18)
**Rnds 11–13** dc (3 rnds)
**Rnd 14** (dc4, dc2tog) 3 times (15)
**Rnd 15** (dc3, dc2tog) 3 times (12)
**Rnd 16** (dc2tog) 6 times (6)

## HEAD

Working in Fudge
Begin by dc6 into ring
**Rnd 1** (dc2 into next st) 6 times (12)
**Rnd 2** (dc1, dc2 into next st) 6 times (18)
**Rnd 3** (dc2, dc2 into next st) 6 times (24)
**Rnds 4–6** dc (3 rnds)
**Rnd 7** (dc2, dc2tog) 6 times (18)
**Rnd 10** dc
**Rnd 11** dc3, (dc2tog) twice, dc5, (dc2tog) twice, dc2 (14)
**Rnd 12** dc3, dc2tog, dc5, dc2tog, dc2 (12)
**Rnd 13** (dc2, dc2tog) 3 times (9)
**Rnd 14** (dc1, dc2tog) 3 times (6)

## LEGS (make four)

Working in Fudge
Begin by dc6 into ring
**Rnd 1** (dc2 into next st) 6 times (12)
**Rnds 2–3** dc (2 rnds)
**Rnd 4** (dc1, dc2tog) 4 times (8)
**Rnds 5–12** dc (8 rnds)
Stuff end and sew flat across top to close.

## EARS (make two)

Working in Fudge
Begin by dc4 into ring
**Rnds 1–2** dc (2 rnds)
Do not stuff.

## SPIKES

Working in Cocoa
Cover the back working ch5 SLIP STITCH CHAINS (see
page 39) with two SLIP STITCH TRAVERSE (see page 39)
sts between.

Finish by sewing eyes and nose into place with Black yarn.

## SLIP STITCH TRAVERSE

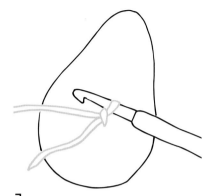

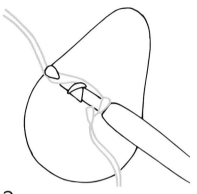

1 Insert the hook into the fabric around a stitch or row.

2 Yarn over and pull through the stitch and all loops on the hook (one slip stitch made).

3 Repeat in desired direction, moving across the surface of the fabric and adding slip st chains as instructed in pattern.

## SLIP STITCH CHAINS

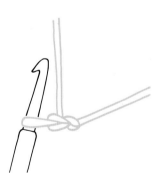

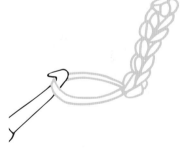

1 Insert the hook through the fabric at the desired position, yarn over and pull through the fabric.

2 Chain the number of stitches stated in the pattern.

3 Working back down the chain, insert the hook into the next stitch, yarn over and pull through the stitch and the loop on the hook (one slip stitch made). Continue slip stitching down the chain, ending with just one loop on the hook.

# GOOSE

**BODY/HEAD**
Working in Oatmeal
Begin by dc6 into ring
**Rnd 1** (dc2 into next st) 6 times (12 sts)
**Rnd 2** (dc1, dc2 into next st) 6 times (18)
**Rnd 3** (dc2, dc2 into next st) 6 times (24)
**Rnd 4** (dc3, dc2 into next st) 6 times (30)
**Rnds 5–12** dc (8 rnds)
**Rnd 13** (dc3, dc2tog) 6 times (24)
**Rnd 14** (dc2tog) 12 times (12)
**Rnd 15** (dc2tog) 6 times (6)
**Rnds 16–18** dc (3 rnds)
**Rnd 19** (dc2 into next st) 6 times (12)
**Rnd 20** (dc2 into next st) 12 times (24)
**Rnd 21** (dc3, dc2 into next st) 6 times (30)
**Rnds 22–24** dc (3 rnds)
**Rnd 25** (dc3, dc2tog) 6 times (24)
**Rnd 26** (dc2, dc2tog) 6 times (18)
**Rnd 27** (dc1, dc2tog) 6 times (12)
**Rnd 28** (dc2tog) 6 times (6)

**LEGS** (make two)
Working in Yellow
Ch5 and sl st to join into a circle
**Rnds 1–4** dc (4 rnds)
**Rnd 5** (dc2 into next st) 5 times (10)
**Rnd 6** dc
**Rnd 7** (dc4, dc2 into next st) twice (12)
**Rnd 8** (dc5, dc2 into next st) twice (14)
**Rnd 9** (dc6, dc2 into next st) twice (16)
**Rnd 10** dc
Fold flat and dc across edge to close (see page 42)
Do not stuff.

**WINGS** (make two)
Working in Oatmeal
Begin by dc6 into ring
**Rnd 1** (dc2 into next st) 6 times (12)
**Rnd 2** dc
**Rnd 3** (dc4, dc2tog) twice (10)
**Rnd 4** (dc3, dc2tog) twice (8)
**Rnd 5** (dc2, dc2tog) twice (6)
**Rnd 6** (dc1, dc2tog) twice (4)
Do not stuff.

**BEAK**
Working in Yellow
Begin by dc6 into ring
**Rnd 1** (dc2 into next st) 6 times (12)
**Rnds 2–4** dc (3 rnds)
**Rnd 5** (dc2, dc2tog) 3 times (9)
**Rnd 6** (dc2, dc2 into next st) 3 times (12)
**Rnd 7** (dc3, dc2 into next st) 3 times (15)
Do not stuff.

Finish by sewing eyes into place with Black yarn.

## CHAIN AND THEN SLIP STITCH TO JOIN INTO A CIRCLE

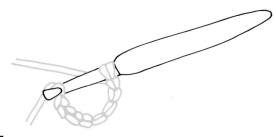 

1 Chain the stated number of stitches, then insert the hook into the back of the stitch closest to the slipknot, ensuring not to twist the stitches.

2 Yarn over the hook.

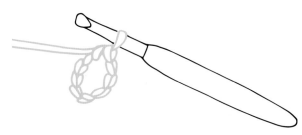

3 Pull the yarn through the stitch and the loop on the hook in one motion.

# FROG

**BODY/HEAD**

Begin by dc6 into ring

**Rnd 1** (dc1, dc2 into next st) 3 times (9 sts)

**Rnd 2** (dc2, dc2 into next st) 3 times (12)

**Rnd 3** (dc2 into next st) twice, dc4, (dc2 into next st) twice, dc4 (16)

**Rnd 4** dc1, (dc2 into next st) twice, dc6, (dc2 into next st) twice, dc5 (20)

**Rnds 5–7** dc (3 rnds)

**Rnd 8** dc2tog, dc6, (dc2tog) twice, dc6, dc2tog (16)

**Rnd 9** dc

**Rnd 10** (dc2tog, dc6) twice (14)

**Rnd 11** (dc5, dc2tog) twice (12)

**Rnd 12** (dc2, dc2tog) 3 times (9)

**Rnd 13** (dc1, dc2tog) 3 times (6)

**Rnd 14** (dc2 into next st) 6 times (12)

**Rnd 15** (dc1, dc2 into next st) 6 times (18)

**Rnd 16** (dc5, dc2 into next st) 3 times (21)

**Rnds 17–18** dc (2 rnds)

**Rnd 19** dc4, (dc2tog) 4 times, dc9 (17)

**Rnd 20** (dc1, dc2tog) 5 times, dc2 (12)

**Rnd 21** (dc2tog) 6 times (6)

**LEGS** (make four)

Ch6 and sl st to join into a circle

**Rnds 1–6** dc (6 rnds)

**Rnd 7** dc2tog, dc4 (5)

Onto end of leg work four toes using
   SLIP STITCH CHAINS (see page 39) as follows:

**Toe 1** ch4, sl st back down ch

**Toe 2** ch5, sl st back down ch

**Toe 3** ch6, sl st back down ch

**Toe 4** ch5, sl st back down ch

Do not stuff.

**EYES** (make two)

Begin by dc6 into ring

**Rnds 1–2** dc (2 rnds)

Sew into place.

Finish by sewing pupils into place with Black yarn.

# FANTASY FARM

What will you have on your farm? Fill your
crocheted fields with all your favourite breeds
of sheep (and have as many border collies to
round them up as you fancy!).

# CHICK

**BODY/HEAD**
Working in Yellow
Begin by dc6 into ring
**Rnd 1** (dc2 into next st) 6 times (12 sts)
**Rnd 2** (dc1, dc2 into next st) 6 times (18)
**Rnd 3** (dc2, dc2 into next st) 6 times (24)
**Rnd 4** (dc3, dc2 into next st) 6 times (30)
**Rnds 5–12** dc (8 rnds)
**Rnd 13** (dc3, dc2tog) 6 times (24)
**Rnd 14** (dc2tog) 12 times (12)
**Rnd 15** (dc2tog) 6 times (6)
**Rnd 16** (dc2 into next st) 6 times (12)
**Rnd 17** (dc2 into next st) 12 times (24)
**Rnd 18** (dc3, dc2 into next st) 6 times (30)
**Rnds 19–21** dc (3 rnds)
**Rnd 22** (dc3, dc2tog) 6 times (24)
**Rnd 23** (dc2, dc2tog) 6 times (18)
**Rnd 24** (dc1, dc2tog) 6 times (12)
**Rnd 25** (dc2tog) 6 times (6)

**LEGS** (make two)
Working in Camel
Ch4 and sl st to join into a circle
**Rnds 1–3** dc (3 rnds)
**Rnd 4** (dc1, dc2 into next st) twice (6)
**Rnd 5** (dc2 into next st) 6 times (12)
Split into three rnds of 4 sts (see page 51) and work
    each as follows:
**Rnds 1–4** dc (4 rnds)
Do not stuff.

**WINGS** (make two)
Working in Yellow
Begin by dc6 into ring
**Rnd 1** (dc2 into next st) 6 times (12)
**Rnd 2** dc
**Rnd 3** (dc4, dc2tog) twice (10)
**Rnd 4** (dc3, dc2tog) twice (8)
**Rnd 5** (dc2, dc2tog) twice (6)
**Rnd 6** (dc1, dc2tog) twice (4)
Do not stuff.

**BEAK**
Working in Camel
Ch8 and sl st to join into a circle
**Rnds 1–2** dc (2 rnds)
**Rnd 3** (dc2tog) 4 times (4)
Stuff lightly and sew into position.

**TAIL**
Working in Yellow
Work three ch7 SLIP STITCH CHAINS (see page 39)
    into tail position.

Finish by sewing eyes into place with Black yarn.

## SPLITTING THE ROUND

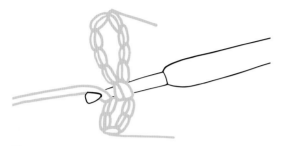

1 Count back the required number of stitches from your hook to split the round as instructed in the pattern. Cross the round and double crochet into this stitch from the right side of the fabric to create two smaller rounds.

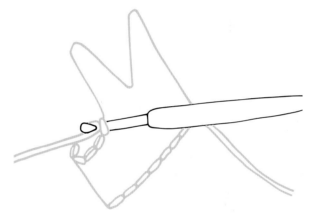

2 Work the stitches on the first smaller round as instructed. Once completed, rejoin the yarn and work the other smaller rounds.

# DONKEY

## BODY
Working in Mushroom
Begin by dc6 into ring
Rnd 1 (dc2 into next st) 6 times (12 sts)
Rnd 2 (dc1, dc2 into next st) 6 times (18)
Rnd 3 (dc2, dc2 into next st) 6 times (24)
Rnds 4–8 dc (5 rnds)
Rnd 9 dc9, (dc2tog) 3 times, dc9 (21)
Rnd 10 (dc5, dc2tog) 3 times (18)
Rnds 11–13 dc (3 rnds)
Rnd 14 (dc4, dc2tog) 3 times (15)
Rnd 15 (dc3, dc2tog) 3 times (12)
Rnd 16 (dc2tog) 6 times (6)

## HEAD
Working in Mushroom
Begin by dc6 into ring
Rnd 1 (dc2 into next st) 6 times (12)
Rnd 2 (dc1, dc2 into next st) 6 times (18)
Rnd 3 (dc2, dc2 into next st) 6 times (24)
Rnds 4–6 dc (3 rnds)
Rnd 7 (dc2, dc2tog) 6 times (18)
Rnd 8 (dc1, dc2tog) 6 times (12)
Rnd 9 dc
Change to Oatmeal
Rnd 10 dc
Rnd 11 (dc3, dc2 into next st) 3 times (15)
Rnd 12 (dc1, dc2tog) 5 times (10)
Rnd 13 (dc2tog) 5 times (5)

## LEGS (make four)
Working in Oatmeal
Begin by dc6 into ring
Rnd 1 (dc2 into next st) 6 times (12)
Rnd 2 dc

Change to Mushroom
Rnd 3 dc
Rnd 4 (dc1, dc2tog) 4 times (8)
Rnds 5–12 dc (8 rnds)
Stuff end and sew flat across top to close.

## EARS (make two)
Working in Mushroom
Begin by dc6 into ring
Rnds 1–2 dc (2 rnds)
Rnd 3 dc2tog, dc4 (5)
Rnd 4 dc2tog, dc3 (4)
Do not stuff.

## TAIL
Working in Mushroom
Work one ch3 SLIP STITCH CHAIN (see page 39) into tail position then work two ch4 CHAIN LOOPS (see page 33) onto the end.

## MANE
Working in Mushroom
Work ch6 CHAIN LOOPS (see page 33) up the back of the head and between the ears.

Finish by sewing eyes into place with Black yarn.

## CHAIN TAIL

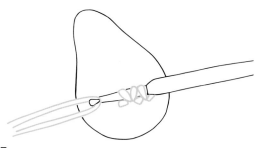

1 Insert the hook through the fabric around a stitch and yarn over with two strands of yarn held together.

2 Chain the number of stitches stated in the pattern, holding all four strands together.

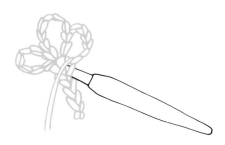

3 Finish the tail by working loops of single-strand chains onto the end with the number of stitches stated in the pattern.

# THE NEXT STEP: CHANGING COLOUR

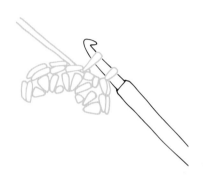

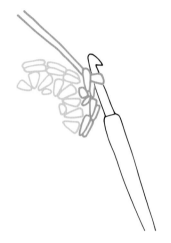

1   Insert the hook through the next stitch, yarn over and pull through the stitch (two loops on hook).

2   Yarn over with the new colour and complete the double crochet stitch with this new yarn.

3   Continue with this new yarn, leaving the original yarn at the back of the work. Cut the original yarn if this is a one-off colour change, or run it along the back of the fabric if returning to it later.

# GOAT

## BODY
Working in Silver
Begin by dc6 into ring
**Rnd 1** (dc2 into next st) 6 times (12 sts)
**Rnd 2** (dc1, dc2 into next st) 6 times (18)
**Rnd 3** (dc2, dc2 into next st) 6 times (24)
**Rnds 4–8** dc (5 rnds)
**Rnd 9** dc9, (dc2tog) 3 times, dc9 (21)
**Rnd 10** (dc5, dc2tog) 3 times (18)
**Rnds 11–13** dc (3 rnds)
**Rnd 14** (dc4, dc2tog) 3 times (15)
**Rnd 15** (dc3, dc2tog) 3 times (12)
**Rnd 16** (dc2tog) 6 times (6)

## HEAD
Working in Silver
Begin by dc6 into ring
**Rnd 1** (dc2 into next st) 6 times (12)
**Rnd 2** (dc1, dc2 into next st) 6 times (18)
**Rnd 3** (dc2, dc2 into next st) 6 times (24)
**Rnds 4–6** dc (3 rnds)
**Rnd 7** (dc2, dc2tog) 6 times (18)
Change to Cream
**Rnd 8** (dc1, dc2tog) 6 times (12)
**Rnds 9–10** dc (2 rnds)
**Rnd 11** (dc2tog) 6 times (6)

## LEGS (make four)
Working in Cream
Begin by dc6 into ring
**Rnd 1** (dc2 into next st) 6 times (12)
**Rnds 2–3** dc (2 rnds)
**Rnd 4** (dc1, dc2tog) 4 times (8)
**Rnd 5** dc

Change to Silver
**Rnds 6–12** dc (7 rnds)
Stuff end and sew flat across top to close.

## EARS (make two)
Working in Silver
Begin by dc6 into ring
**Rnd 1** (dc2, dc2 into next st) twice (8)
**Rnds 2–5** dc (4 rnds)
**Rnd 6** (dc2tog, dc2) twice (6)
**Rnd 7** (dc2tog, dc1) twice (4)
**Rnd 8** (dc2tog) twice (2)
Do not stuff.

## HORNS
Working in Cream
Work two ch3 SLIP STITCH CHAINS (see page 39) on the
    top of head between ears.

## BEARD
Working in Cream
Work three ch5 CHAIN LOOPS (see page 33) under chin.

## TAIL
Working in Silver
Create CHAIN TAIL (see page 55): sl st into tail position, ch3,
    then work three ch3 loops onto end.

Finish by sewing eyes into place with Black yarn.

# PONY

## BODY
Working in Camel
Begin by dc6 into ring
Rnd 1 (dc2 into next st) 6 times (12 sts)
Rnd 2 (dc1, dc2 into next st) 6 times (18)
Rnd 3 (dc2, dc2 into next st) 6 times (24)
Rnds 4–8 dc (5 rnds)
Rnd 9 dc9, (dc2tog) 3 times, dc9 (21)
Rnd 10 (dc5, dc2tog) 3 times (18)
Rnds 11–13 dc (3 rnds)
Rnd 14 (dc4, dc2tog) 3 times (15)
Rnd 15 (dc3, dc2tog) 3 times (12)
Rnd 16 (dc2tog) 6 times (6)

## HEAD
Working in Camel
Begin by dc6 into ring
Rnd 1 (dc2 into next st) 6 times (12)
Rnd 2 (dc1, dc2 into next st) 6 times (18)
Rnd 3 (dc2, dc2 into next st) 6 times (24)
Rnds 4–6 dc (3 rnds)
Rnd 7 (dc2, dc2tog) 6 times (18)
Rnd 8 (dc1, dc2tog) 6 times (12)
Rnds 9–10 dc (2 rnds)
Rnd 11 (dc3, dc2 into next st) 3 times (15)
Rnd 12 (dc1, dc2tog) 5 times (10)
Rnd 13 (dc2tog) 5 times (5)

## LEGS (make four)
Working in Cream
Begin by dc6 into ring
Rnd 1 (dc2 into next st) 6 times (12)
Rnds 2–3 dc (2 rnds)
Rnd 4 (dc1, dc2tog) 4 times (8)

Change to Camel
Rnds 5–12 dc (8 rnds)
Stuff end and sew flat across top to close.

## EARS (make two)
Working in Camel
Begin by dc6 into ring
Rnd 1 dc
Rnd 2 dc2tog, dc4 (5)
Rnd 3 dc2tog, dc3 (4)
Do not stuff.

## TAIL
Working in Cream
Work three ch15 CHAIN LOOPS (see page 33) into
    tail position.

## MANE
Working in Cream
Work ch8 CHAIN LOOPS (see page 33) up the back of the
    head and between the ears.

Finish by sewing eyes into place with Black yarn.

# BADGER

## BODY

Working in Charcoal
Begin by dc6 into ring
**Rnd 1** (dc2 into next st) 6 times (12 sts)
**Rnd 2** (dc1, dc2 into next st) 6 times (18)
**Rnd 3** (dc2, dc2 into next st) 6 times (24)
**Rnds 4–8** dc (5 rnds)
**Rnd 9** dc9, (dc2tog) 3 times, dc9 (21)
**Rnd 10** (dc5, dc2tog) 3 times (18)
**Rnds 11–13** dc (3 rnds)
**Rnd 14** (dc4, dc2tog) 3 times (15)
**Rnd 15** (dc3, dc2tog) 3 times (12)
**Rnd 16** (dc2tog) 6 times (6)

## HEAD

Working in Charcoal
Begin by dc6 into ring
**Rnd 1** (dc2 into next st) 6 times (12)
**Rnd 2** (dc1, dc2 into next st) 6 times (18)
**Rnd 3** (dc2, dc2 into next st) 6 times (24)
**Rnds 4–5** dc (2 rnds)
Change to Cream
**Rnds 6–7** dc (2 rnds)
**Rnd 8** (dc6, dc2tog) 3 times (21)
**Rnd 9** (dc5, dc2tog) 3 times (18)
**Rnd 10** (dc4, dc2tog) 3 times (15)
**Rnd 11** (dc3, dc2tog) 3 times (12)
**Rnd 12** (dc2, dc2tog) 3 times (9)
**Rnd 13** (dc1, dc2tog) 3 times (6)

## LEGS (make four)

Working in Charcoal
Begin by dc6 into ring

**Rnd 1** (dc2 into next st) 6 times (12)
**Rnds 2–3** dc (2 rnds)
**Rnd 4** (dc1, dc2tog) 4 times (8)
**Rnds 5–12** dc (8 rnds)
Stuff end and sew flat across top to close.

## EARS (make two)

Working in Cream
Begin by dc6 into ring
Change to Charcoal
**Rnd 1** (dc1, dc2 into next st) 3 times (9)
**Rnd 2** dc
**Rnd 3** (dc1, dc2tog) 3 times (6)
Do not stuff.

## TAIL

Working in Charcoal
Begin by dc6 into ring
**Rnds 1–2** dc
Sew into position without stuffing.

## FACIAL MARKINGS (make two)

Using a sewing needle with two strands of Charcoal yarn
held together, sew two large stitches across four rnds
from colour change rnd.

Finish by sewing eyes and nose into place with Black yarn.

# MOLE

## BODY
Working in Charcoal
Begin by dc6 into ring
**Rnd 1** (dc2 into next st) 6 times (12 sts)
**Rnd 2** (dc1, dc2 into next st) 6 times (18)
**Rnd 3** (dc2, dc2 into next st) 6 times (24)
**Rnds 4-8** dc (5 rnds)
**Rnd 9** dc9, (dc2tog) 3 times, dc9 (21)
**Rnd 10** (dc5, dc2tog) 3 times (18)
**Rnds 11-13** dc (3 rnds)
**Rnd 14** (dc4, dc2tog) 3 times (15)
**Rnd 15** (dc3, dc2tog) 3 times (12)
**Rnd 16** (dc2tog) 6 times (6)

## HEAD
Working in Charcoal
Begin by dc6 into ring
**Rnd 1** (dc2 into next st) 6 times (12)
**Rnd 2** (dc1, dc2 into next st) 6 times (18)
**Rnd 3** (dc2, dc2 into next st) 6 times (24)
**Rnds 4-6** dc (3 rnds)
**Rnd 7** (dc2, dc2tog) 6 times (18)
**Rnd 8** (dc4, dc2tog) 3 times (15)
**Rnd 9** (dc3, dc2tog) 3 times (12)
**Rnd 10** (dc2, dc2tog) 3 times (9)
**Rnd 11** dc
Change to Oatmeal
**Rnds 12-13** dc (2 rnds)
**Rnd 14** (dc1, dc2tog) 3 times (6)

## FRONT LEGS (make two)
Working in Charcoal
Ch8 and sl st to join into a circle
**Rnds 1-8** dc (8 rnds)
Change to Oatmeal
**Rnd 9** (dc1, dc2 into next st) 4 times (12)
**Rnds 10-14** dc (5 rnds)
Dc across top to close, turn, (ch3, dc2 back down ch, sl st1)
   3 times

## BACK LEGS (make two)
Working in Charcoal
Begin by dc6 into ring
**Rnd 1** (dc2 into next st) 6 times (12)
**Rnds 2-3** dc (2 rnds)
**Rnd 4** (dc1, dc2tog) 4 times (8)
**Rnds 5-12** dc (8 rnds)
Stuff end and sew flat across top to close.

Finish by sewing eyes into place with Black yarn.

# DORSET DOWN SHEEP

## BODY

Working in Cream
Begin by dc6 into ring
**Rnd 1** (dc2 into next st) 6 times (12 sts)
**Rnd 2** (dc1, dc2 into next st) 6 times (18)
**Rnd 3** (dc2, dc2 into next st) 6 times (24)
**Rnds 4–8** dc (5 rnds)
**Rnd 9** dc9, (dc2tog) 3 times, dc9 (21)
**Rnd 10** (dc5, dc2tog) 3 times (18)
**Rnds 11–13** dc (3 rnds)
**Rnd 14** (dc4, dc2tog) 3 times (15)
**Rnd 15** (dc3, dc2tog) 3 times (12)
**Rnd 16** (dc2tog) 6 times (6)

## HEAD

Working in Cream
Begin by dc6 into ring
**Rnd 1** (dc2 into next st) 6 times (12)
**Rnd 2** (dc1, dc2 into next st) 6 times (18)
**Rnd 3** (dc2, dc2 into next st) 6 times (24)
**Rnds 4–6** dc (3 rnds)
**Rnd 7** (dc2tog) 3 times, dc18 (21)
Change to Mushroom
**Rnd 8** (dc5, dc2tog) 3 times (18)
**Rnd 9** dc
**Rnd 10** (dc4, dc2tog) 3 times (15)
**Rnd 11** (dc3, dc2tog) 3 times (12)
**Rnd 12** (dc2tog) 6 times (6)

## LEGS (make four)

Working in Mushroom
Begin by dc6 into ring
**Rnd 1** (dc2 into next st) 6 times (12)
**Rnds 2–3** dc (2 rnds)
**Rnd 4** (dc1, dc2tog) 4 times (8)
**Rnds 5–12** dc (8 rnds)
Stuff end and sew flat across top to close.

## EARS (make two)

Working in Mushroom
Begin by dc6 into ring
**Rnds 1–2** dc (2 rnds)
Do not stuff.

## TAIL

Working in Cream
Begin by dc5 into ring
**Rnds 1–8** dc (8 rnds)
Do not stuff.

## FLEECE

Working in Cream
Work ch5 CHAIN LOOPS (see page 33) all over the body,
    leaving bottom plain to ensure balance when sitting.

Finish by sewing eyes into place with Black yarn.

# FOX

## BODY

Working in Fudge
Begin by dc6 into ring
Rnd 1 (dc2 into next st) 6 times (12 sts)
Rnd 2 (dc1, dc2 into next st) 6 times (18)
Rnd 3 (dc2, dc2 into next st) 6 times (24)
Rnds 4-8 dc (5 rnds)
Rnd 9 dc9, (dc2tog) 3 times, dc9 (21)
Rnd 10 (dc5, dc2tog) 3 times (18)
Rnds 11-13 dc (3 rnds)
Rnd 14 (dc4, dc2tog) 3 times (15)
Rnd 15 (dc3, dc2tog) 3 times (12)
Rnd 16 (dc2tog) 6 times (6)

## HEAD

Working in Fudge
Begin by dc6 into ring
Rnd 1 (dc2 into next st) 6 times (12)
Rnd 2 (dc1, dc2 into next st) 6 times (18)
Rnd 3 (dc2, dc2 into next st) 6 times (24)
Rnds 4-6 dc (3 rnds)
Rnds 7-8 dc12 Fudge, dc12 Cream (2 rnds)
Rnd 9 (dc2, dc2tog) 3 times Fudge, (dc2, dc2tog) 3 times Cream (18)
Rnd 10 dc10 Fudge, dc8 Cream
Rnd 11 dc3, (dc2tog) twice, dc3 Fudge, dc2, (dc2tog) twice, dc2 Cream (14)
Rnd 12 dc3, dc2tog, dc3 Fudge, dc2, dc2tog, dc2 Cream (12)
Continue in Cream
Rnd 13 (dc2, dc2tog) 3 times (9)
Rnd 14 (dc1, dc2tog) 3 times (6)

## LEGS (make four)

Working in Fudge
Begin by dc6 into ring
Rnd 1 (dc2 into next st) 6 times (12)
Rnds 2-3 dc (2 rnds)
Rnd 4 (dc1, dc2tog) 4 times (8)
Rnds 5-12 dc (8 rnds)
Stuff end and sew flat across top to close.

## EARS (make two)

Working in Fudge
Begin by dc6 into ring
Rnd 1 (dc1, dc2 into next st) 3 times (9)
Rnds 2-4 dc (3 rnds)
Rnd 5 (dc1, dc2tog) 3 times (6)
Rnd 6 (dc2tog) 3 times (3)
Do not stuff.

## TAIL

Working in Fudge
Ch6 and sl st to join into a circle
Rnds 1-3 dc (3 rnds)
Rnd 4 dc2 into next st, dc5 (7)
Rnds 5-7 dc (3 rnds)
Rnd 8 dc2 into next st, dc6 (8)
Rnd 9 dc
Change to Cream
Rnds 10-11 dc (2 rnds)
Rnd 12 (dc2, dc2tog) twice (6)
Rnd 13 (dc2tog) 3 times (3)
Sew into position without stuffing.

Finish by sewing eyes and nose into place with Black yarn.

# ROBIN

**BODY/HEAD**
Working in Cream
Begin by dc6 into ring
**Rnd 1** (dc2 into next st) 6 times (12 sts)
**Rnd 2** (dc1, dc2 into next st) 6 times (18)
**Rnd 3** (dc2, dc2 into next st) 6 times (24)
**Rnd 4** (dc3, dc2 into next st) 6 times (30)
**Rnds 5–12** dc (8 rnds)
Change to Ruby
**Rnd 13** (dc3, dc2tog) 6 times (24)
**Rnd 14** (dc2tog) 12 times (12)
**Rnd 15** (dc2tog) 6 times (6)
**Rnd 16** (dc2 into next st) 3 times Ruby, (dc2 into next st)
   3 times Stone (12)
**Rnd 17** (dc2 into next st) 6 times Ruby, (dc2 into next st)
   6 times Stone (24)
**Rnd 18** (dc3, dc2 into next st) 3 times Ruby, (dc3, dc2 into
   next st) 3 times Stone (30)
**Rnds 19–21** dc15 Ruby, dc15 Stone (3 rnds)
Continue in Stone
**Rnd 22** (dc3, dc2tog) 6 times (24)
**Rnd 23** (dc2, dc2tog) 6 times (18)
**Rnd 24** (dc1, dc2tog) 6 times (12)
**Rnd 25** (dc2tog) 6 times (6)

**LEGS (MAKE TWO)**
Working in Stone
Begin by dc4 into ring
**Rnds 1–3** dc (3 rnds)
Next, (ch4, turn and sl st back down ch, sl st into next st)
   3 times to create claws.

**WINGS** (make two)
Working in Stone
Begin by dc6 into ring
**Rnd 1** (dc2 into next st) 6 times (12)
**Rnd 2** (dc1, dc2 into next st) 6 times (18)
**Rnds 3–5** dc (3 rnds)
**Rnd 6** (dc1, dc2tog) 6 times (12)
**Rnd 7** (dc2, dc2tog) 3 times (9)
**Rnd 8** (dc1, dc2tog) 3 times (6)
**Rnd 9** dc
Do not stuff.

**BEAK**
Working in Stone
Work one ch4 SLIP STITCH CHAIN (see page 39) for beak.

**TAIL**
Working in Stone
Sl st into tail position, ch10 and work back down ch
   as follows:
tr3, htr3, dc2 (see page 75)
Repeat to make second feather.

Finish by sewing eyes into place with Black yarn.

## HALF TREBLE CROCHET STITCH (HTR)

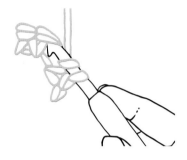

1  Yarn over and insert the hook into the next stitch.

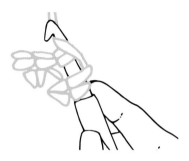

2  Yarn over and pull through the stitch (three loops on hook).

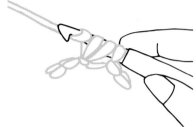

3  Yarn over and pull through all three loops on the hook (one half treble crochet stitch made).

## TREBLE CROCHET STITCH (TR)

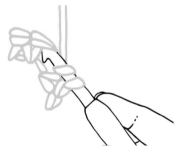

1  Yarn over and insert the hook into the next stitch.

2  Yarn over and pull through the stitch (three loops on hook), then yarn over again and pull through the first two loops on the hook (two loops on hook).

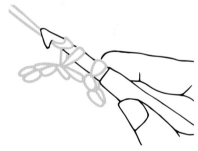

3  Yarn over again and pull through the remaining two loops on the hook (one treble crochet stitch made).

# FRIESIAN COW

## BODY

Working in Black
Begin by dc6 into ring
**Rnd 1** (dc2 into next st) 6 times (12 sts)
**Rnd 2** (dc1, dc2 into next st) 6 times (18)
**Rnd 3** (dc2, dc2 into next st) 6 times (24)
**Rnds 4–7** dc (4 rnds)
Change to Cream
**Rnd 8** dc
**Rnd 9** dc9, (dc2tog) 3 times, dc9 (21)
**Rnd 10** (dc5, dc2tog) 3 times (18)
**Rnds 11–12** dc (2 rnds)
Change to Black
**Rnd 13** dc
**Rnd 14** (dc4, dc2tog) 3 times (15)
**Rnd 15** (dc3, dc2tog) 3 times (12)
**Rnd 16** (dc2tog) 6 times (6)

## HEAD

Working in Black
Begin by dc6 into ring
**Rnd 1** (dc2 into next st) 6 times (12)
**Rnd 2** (dc1, dc2 into next st) 6 times (18)
**Rnd 3** (dc2, dc2 into next st) 6 times (24)
**Rnds 4–6** dc (3 rnds)
**Rnd 7** dc1 Black, dc6 Cream, dc17 Black (24)
**Rnd 8** dc2tog, dc1 Black, dc2 Cream, dc1, dc2tog, dc16 Black (22)
**Rnd 9** dc2tog Black, dc2tog Cream, dc2tog, dc16 Black (19)
**Rnd 10** dc3 Cream, dc2, dc2tog, (dc1, dc2tog) 4 times Black (14)
**Rnd 11** dc1 Black, dc2 Cream, dc1, dc2tog, dc6, dc2tog Black (12)

**Rnd 12** dc1 Black, dc1, dc2 into next st, (dc2, dc2 into next st) 3 times Cream (16)
Continue in Cream
**Rnd 13** dc
**Rnd 14** (dc2tog) 8 times (8)

## LEGS (make four)

Working in Black
Begin by dc6 into ring
**Rnd 1** (dc2 into next st) 6 times (12)
**Rnds 2–3** dc (2 rnds)
Change to Cream
**Rnd 4** (dc1, dc2tog) 4 times (8)
**Rnds 5–12** dc (8 rnds)
Stuff end and sew flat across top to close.

## EARS (make two)

Working in Black
Begin by dc6 into ring
**Rnds 1–3** dc (3 rnds)
Do not stuff.

## TAIL

Working in Black
Sl st into tail position, ch3, then work three ch3 CHAIN LOOPS (see page 33) onto end in Cream.

Finish by sewing eyes into place with Black yarn.

# PHEASANT

COLOURS | FUDGE, RUBY, TEAL, OATMEAL, CAMEL, CHESTNUT

**BODY/HEAD**
Working in Fudge
Begin by dc6 into ring
**Rnd 1** (dc2 into next st) 6 times (12 sts)
**Rnd 2** (dc1, dc2 into next st) 6 times (18)
**Rnd 3** (dc2, dc2 into next st) 6 times (24)
**Rnd 4** (dc3, dc2 into next st) 6 times (30)
**Rnds 5–12** dc (8 rnds)
**Rnd 13** (dc3, dc2tog) 6 times (24)
**Rnd 14** (dc2tog) 12 times (12)
**Rnd 15** (dc2tog) 6 times (6)
**Rnd 16** (dc2 into next st) 3 times Ruby, (dc2 into next st) 3 times Teal (12)
**Rnd 17** (dc2 into next st) 6 times Ruby, (dc2 into next st) 6 times Teal (24)
**Rnd 18** (dc3, dc2 into next st) 3 times Ruby, (dc3, dc2 into next st) 3 times Teal (30)
**Rnds 19–21** dc15 Ruby, dc15 Teal (3 rnds)
Continue in Teal
**Rnd 22** (dc3, dc2tog) 6 times (24)
**Rnd 23** (dc2, dc2tog) 6 times (18)
**Rnd 24** (dc1, dc2tog) 6 times (12)
**Rnd 25** (dc2tog) 6 times (6)

**LEGS** (make two)
Working in Oatmeal
Ch4 and sl st to join into a circle
**Rnds 1–3** dc (3 rnds)
**Rnd 4** (dc1, dc2 into next st) twice (6)
**Rnd 5** (dc2 into next st) 6 times (12)
Split into three rnds of 4 sts and work each as follows:
**Rnds 1–4** dc (4 rnds)
Do not stuff.

**WINGS** (make two)
Working in Camel with a random Chestnut st approximately every fifth st.
Begin by dc6 into ring
**Rnd 1** (dc2 into next st) 6 times (12)
**Rnd 2** dc
**Rnd 3** (dc4, dc2tog) twice (10)
**Rnd 4** (dc3, dc2tog) twice (8)
**Rnd 5** (dc2, dc2tog) twice (6)
**Rnd 6** (dc1, dc2tog) twice (4)
Do not stuff.

**BEAK**
Working in Oatmeal
Work one ch3 SLIP STITCH CHAIN (see page 39) into beak position.

**TAIL**
Working Fudge
Sl st at poisiton of tail and ch10
Turn and work back down ch:
dc3 into next st, dc3, sl st5
Repeat to make second feather.

Finish by sewing eyes into place with Black yarn.

# BAT

## BODY
Begin by dc6 into ring
**Rnd 1** (dc2 into next st) 6 times (12 sts)
**Rnd 2** (dc1, dc2 into next st) 6 times (18)
**Rnd 3** (dc2, dc2 into next st) 6 times (24)
**Rnds 4–8** dc (5 rnds)
**Rnd 9** dc9, (dc2tog) 3 times, dc9 (21)
**Rnd 10** (dc5, dc2tog) 3 times (18)
**Rnds 11–13** dc (3 rnds)
**Rnd 14** (dc4, dc2tog) 3 times (15)
**Rnd 15** (dc3, dc2tog) 3 times (12)
**Rnd 16** (dc2tog) 6 times (6)

## HEAD
Begin by dc6 into ring
**Rnd 1** (dc2 into next st) 6 times (12)
**Rnd 2** (dc1, dc2 into next st) 6 times (18)
**Rnd 3** (dc2, dc2 into next st) 6 times (24)
**Rnds 4–7** dc (4 rnds)
**Rnd 8** (dc2tog) 12 times (12)
**Rnd 9** dc
**Rnd 10** (dc2tog) 6 times (6)

## FRONT LEGS (make two)
Begin by dc6 into ring
**Rnd 1** (dc2 into next st) 6 times (12)
**Rnds 2–3** dc (2 rnds)
**Rnd 4** (dc2tog) 6 times (6)
**Rnds 5–19** dc (15 rnds)
Stuff end and sew top closed.

## BACK LEGS (make two)
Begin by dc6 into ring
**Rnd 1** (dc2 into next st) 6 times (12)
**Rnds 2–3** dc (2 rnds)

**Rnd 4** (dc1, dc2tog) 4 times (8)
**Rnds 5–10** dc (6 rnds)
Stuff end and sew flat across top to close.

## EARS (make two)
Ch8 and sl st to join into a circle
**Rnd 1** dc
**Rnd 2** dc2tog, dc6 (7)
**Rnd 3** dc2tog, dc5 (6)
**Rnd 4** dc2tog, dc4 (5)
**Rnd 5** dc2tog, dc3 (4)
Do not stuff.

## WINGS (make two)
Once stuffed and sewn together, SLIP STITCH TRAVERSE (see page 39) 3 sts underneath armpit.
Work along these 3 sts in rows as follows:
**Row 1** turn, dc3, sl st into next st down leg (3)
**Row 2** turn, dc3, sl st into next st down body
**Row 3** turn, dc2 into next st, dc2, sl st into next st down leg (4)
**Row 4** turn, dc2 into next st, dc3, sl st into next st down body (5)
**Rows 5–9** Continue working back and forth down length of body, increasing 1 st at beginning of each row until wing connects bottom of body to 'wrist' (5 rnds)

Finish by sewing eyes and nostrils into place with Black yarn.

## WORKING WINGS

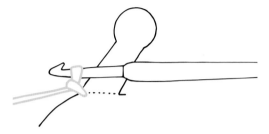 

1 After stuffing and sewing the animal together, insert the hook into the fabric around the central stitch of the 'armpit', yarn over and pull through.

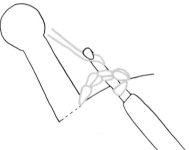

2 Slip stitch traverse three stitches underneath the armpit.

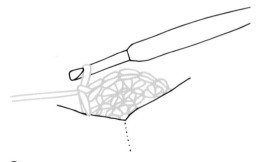

3 Now work along three stitches backwards and forwards in rows following the increase pattern.

# SWALEDALE SHEEP

**BODY**
Working in Charcoal, work as for Sheep (page 30)

**HEAD**
Working in Charcoal
Begin by dc6 into ring
Rnd 1 (dc2 into next st) 6 times (12)
Rnd 2 (dc1, dc2 into next st) 6 times (18)
Rnd 3 (dc2, dc2 into next st) 6 times (24)
Rnds 4–6 dc (3 rnds)
Rnd 7 (dc2tog) 3 times, dc18 (21)
Rnd 8 (dc5, dc2tog) 3 times (18)
Change to Cream
Rnd 9 dc
Rnd 10 (dc4, dc2tog) 3 times (15)
Rnd 11 (dc3, dc2tog) 3 times (12)
Rnd 12 (dc2tog) 6 times (6)

**LEGS** (make four)
Working in Charcoal
Begin by dc6 into ring
Rnd 1 (dc2 into next st) 6 times (12)
Rnds 2–3 dc (2 rnds)
Change to Cream
Rnd 4 (dc1, dc2tog) 4 times (8)
Continue working 1 st Charcoal and 1 st Cream on odd
    rnds, and working in Cream on even rnds
Rnds 5–12 dc (8 rnds)
Stuff end and sew flat across top to close.

**HORNS** (make two)
Working in Camel
Begin by dc4 into ring
Continue working in back loop only
Rnd 1 (dc2 into next st) 4 times (8)
Rnds 2–4 dc (3 rnds)

Rnd 5 dc2tog, dc6 (7)
Rnd 6 dc
Rnd 7 dc2tog, dc5 (6)
Rnd 8 dc
Rnd 9 dc2tog, dc4 (5)
Rnd 10 dc
Rnd 11 dc2tog, dc3 (4)
Rnd 12 dc

**EYES** (make two)
Working in Cream
Dc6 into ring

**EARS** (make two)
Working in Charcoal
Begin by dc5 into ring
Rnd 1–3 dc (3 rnds)
Do not stuff.

**TAIL**
Working in Charcoal
Begin by dc5 into ring
Rnds 1–3 dc (3 rnds)

**FLEECE**
Working in Cream work ch6 CHAIN LOOPS
    (see page 33) all over body.
Finish by sewing pupils and nose into place with
    Black yarn.

## WORKING INTO BACK LOOPS ONLY

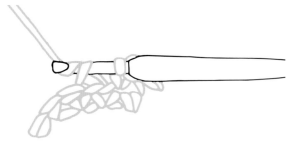

Insert the hook in between the two strands of the 'V' of the next stitch so that you are working under the back loop only. This leaves the front loop to form a lined texture on the surface of the right side of the fabric.

## SEWING ON A PIECE

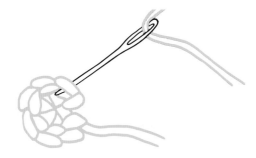

1. Pin if necessary.
2. Backstitch around the edge.
3. Fasten off by sewing through the piece and around a stitch.

Create a different texture on your fabric by working only the back loop on the horns.

# SNAIL

## BODY/HEAD

Working in Stone

Begin by dc4 into ring

**Rnds 1, 3 and 5** dc

**Rnd 2** dc2 into next st, dc3 (5 sts)

**Rnd 4** dc2 into next st, dc4 (6)

**Rnd 6** dc5, dc2 into next st (7)

**Rnd 7** dc2 into next st, dc6 (8)

**Rnd 8** dc

**Rnd 9** dc2 into next st, dc7 (9)

**Rnds 10–12** dc (3 rnds)

**Rnd 13** dc2 into next st, dc8 (10)

**Rnd 14** dc2 into next st, dc9 (11)

Stuff and continue

**Rnd 15** (dc2 into next st) twice, dc3, (dc2tog) twice, dc2 (11)

**Rnd 16** (dc2 into next st) twice, dc1, (dc2tog) 3 times, dc2 (10)

**Rnd 17** dc2 into next st, dc3, (dc2tog) 3 times (8)

**Rnd 18** htr4, (dc2tog) twice (6)

Stuff and continue to tentacles

## TENTACLES

Fold head in half and dc top closed (3)

Ch5, turn and work back down chain as follows:

sl st4, sl st2 through both layers of head, ch5, sl st4 back
down ch

## SHELL

Working in Fudge through back loops only throughout

Ch15 and sl st to join into a circle

**Rnds 1–5** dc (5 rnds)

**Rnd 6** dc2tog, dc13 (14)

**Rnds 7–8** dc (2 rnds)

**Rnd 9** dc2tog, dc12 (13)

**Rnd 10** dc2tog, dc11 (12)

**Rnd 11** dc2tog, dc10 (11)

**Rnd 12** dc2tog, dc9 (10)

**Rnd 13** dc2tog, dc8 (9)

**Rnd 14** dc2tog, dc7 (8)

**Rnd 15** dc2tog, dc6 (7)

**Rnd 16** dc2tog, dc5 (6)

**Rnd 17** dc2tog, dc4 (5)

**Rnds 18–19** dc (2 rnds)

**Rnd 20** dc2tog, dc3 (4)

See page 91 for sewing up instructions.

## SEWING TOGETHER

1. Stuff the shell then curl it around into a spiral and sew through the whole piece to keep in position.
2. Sew shell into position on the body piece.
3. Complete the body piece by adding the eyes in Black onto both tentacle ends.

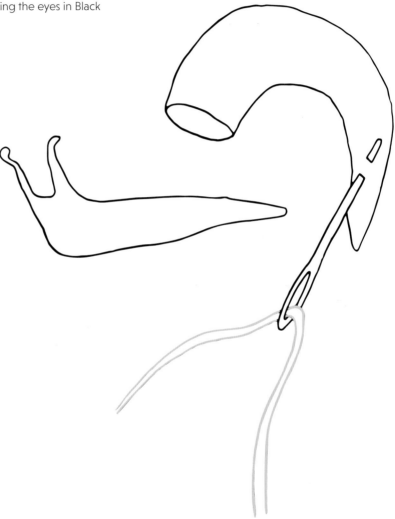

# THE NEXT STEP: LOOP STITCH

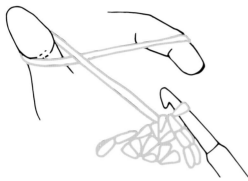

1 Insert the hook through the stitch. Wrap the yarn from front to back over the thumb of your non-hook hand and yarn over with the yarn behind your thumb.

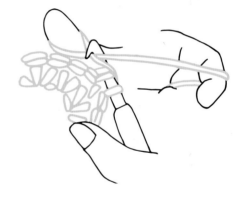

2 Hold the loop on your thumb and complete the double crochet stitch.

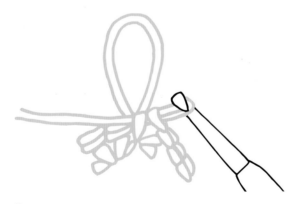

3 Moving your thumb forwards and releasing the loop to position it on the right side of the fabric, work the next stitch to secure the loop in place. Work as often as directed in the pattern.

# SQUIRREL

## BODY

Begin by dc6 into ring
**Rnd 1** (dc2 into next st) 6 times (12 sts)
**Rnd 2** (dc1, dc2 into next st) 6 times (18)
**Rnd 3** (dc2, dc2 into next st) 6 times (24)
**Rnds 4–8** dc (5 rnds)
**Rnd 9** dc9, (dc2tog) 3 times, dc9 (21)
**Rnd 10** (dc5, dc2tog) 3 times (18)
**Rnds 11–13** dc (3 rnds)
**Rnd 14** (dc4, dc2tog) 3 times (15)
**Rnd 15** (dc3, dc2tog) 3 times (12)
**Rnd 16** (dc2tog) 6 times (6)

## HEAD

Begin by dc6 into ring
**Rnd 1** (dc2 into next st) 6 times (12)
**Rnd 2** (dc1, dc2 into next st) 6 times (18)
**Rnd 3** (dc2, dc2 into next st) 6 times (24)
**Rnds 4–6** dc (3 rnds)
**Rnd 7** (dc6, dc2tog) 3 times (21)
**Rnd 8** (dc5, dc2tog) 3 times (18)
**Rnd 9** (dc4, dc2tog) 3 times (15)
**Rnd 10** (dc3, dc2tog) 3 times (12)
**Rnd 11** (dc1, dc2tog) 4 times (8)
**Rnd 12** (dc2tog) 4 times (4)

## LEGS (make four)

Begin by dc6 into ring
**Rnd 1** (dc2 into next st) 6 times (12)
**Rnds 2–3** dc (2 rnds)
**Rnd 4** (dc1, dc2tog) 4 times (8)
**Rnds 5–12** dc (8 rnds)
Stuff end and sew flat across top to close.

## EARS (make two)

Begin by dc6 into ring
**Rnd 1** dc
**Rnd 2** dc2tog, dc4 (5)
**Rnd 3** dc2tog, dc3 (4)
Do not stuff.

## TAIL

Work 1cm LOOP STITCH (see page 93) every
    other st throughout
Begin by dc6 into ring
**Rnd 1** (dc1, dc2 into next st) 3 times (9)
**Rnds 2–16** dc (15 rnds)

Finish by sewing eyes into place with Black yarn.

# BORDER COLLIE

## BODY

Working in Charcoal
Begin by dc6 into ring
**Rnd 1** (dc2 into next st) 6 times (12 sts)
**Rnd 2** (dc1, dc2 into next st) 6 times (18)
**Rnd 3** (dc2, dc2 into next st) 6 times (24)
**Rnds 4–8** dc (5 rnds)
**Rnd 9** dc9, (dc2tog) 3 times, dc9 (21)
**Rnd 10** (dc5, dc2tog) 3 times (18)
**Rnd 11** dc
Work 1cm LOOP STITCH (see page 93) every stitch
    when using Cream
**Rnds 12–13** dc7 Charcoal, dc4 Cream, dc7 Charcoal (2 rnds)
**Rnd 14** dc4, dc2tog, dc2 Charcoal, dc2, dc2tog Cream,
    dc4, dc2tog Charcoal (15)
**Rnd 15** dc3, dc2tog, dc2 Charcoal, dc1, dc2tog Cream,
    dc3, dc2tog Charcoal (12)
Continue in Charcoal
**Rnd 16** (dc2tog) 6 times (6)

## HEAD

Work as body until Rnd 4
**Rnds 4–6** dc (3 rnds)
**Rnd 7** dc2 Charcoal, dc4 Cream, (dc1, dc2tog) 6 times
    Charcoal (18)
**Rnd 8** dc2tog, dc1 Charcoal, dc3 Cream, dc2tog, dc10
    Charcoal (16)
**Rnd 9** dc3 Charcoal, dc1 Cream, (dc1, dc2tog) 4 times
    Charcoal (12)
**Rnd 10** dc3 Charcoal, dc1 Cream, dc8 Charcoal
Continue in Cream
**Rnds 11–12** dc (2 rnds)
**Rnd 13** (dc2, dc2tog) 3 times (9)
**Rnd 14** (dc1, dc2tog) 3 times (6)

## LEGS (make four)

Working in Cream
Begin by dc6 into ring
**Rnd 1** (dc2 into next st) 6 times (12)
**Rnds 2–3** dc (2 rnds)
**Rnd 4** (dc1, dc2tog) 4 times (8)
**Rnds 5–6** dc (2 rnds)
Change to Charcoal
**Rnds 7–12** dc (6 rnds)
Stuff end and sew flat across top to close.

## EARS (make two)

Working in Charcoal
Ch6 and sl st to join into a circle
**Rnd 1** (dc2 into next st) 6 times (12)
**Rnds 2–6** dc (5 rnds)
**Rnd 7** (dc2, dc2tog) 3 times (9)
**Rnd 8** (dc1, dc2tog) 3 times (6)
Sew into position.

## TAIL

Working in Charcoal
Ch5 and sl st to join into a circle
**Rnds 1–3** dc (3 rnds)
Change to Cream and work 1cm LOOP STITCH (see
    page 93) every other st
**Rnd 4** dc2tog, dc3 (4)
**Rnd 5** dc
**Rnd 6** dc2tog, dc2 (3)
Sew into position.

Finish by sewing eyes and nose into place with Black yarn.

# SHIRE HORSE

## BODY

Working in Chestnut
Begin by dc6 into ring
**Rnd 1** (dc2 into next st) 6 times (12 sts)
**Rnd 2** (dc1, dc2 into next st) 6 times (18)
**Rnd 3** (dc2, dc2 into next st) 6 times (24)
**Rnds 4–8** dc (5 rnds)
**Rnd 9** dc9, (dc2tog) 3 times, dc9 (21)
**Rnd 10** (dc5, dc2tog) 3 times (18)
**Rnds 11–13** dc (3 rnds)
**Rnd 14** (dc4, dc2tog) 3 times (15)
**Rnd 15** (dc3, dc2tog) 3 times (12)
**Rnd 16** (dc2tog) 6 times (6)

## HEAD

Working in Chestnut
Begin by dc6 into ring
**Rnd 1** (dc2 into next st) 6 times (12)
**Rnd 2** (dc1, dc2 into next st) 6 times (18)
**Rnd 3** (dc2, dc2 into next st) 6 times (24)
**Rnds 4–6** dc (3 rnds)
**Rnd 7** (dc2, dc2tog) 6 times (18)
**Rnd 8** (dc1, dc2tog) 6 times (12)
Change to Cream
**Rnds 9–10** dc (2 rnds)
**Rnd 11** (dc3, dc2 into next st) 3 times (15)
**Rnd 12** (dc1, dc2tog) 5 times (10)
**Rnd 13** (dc2tog) 5 times (5)

## EARS (make two)

Working in Chestnut
Begin by dc6 into ring
**Rnd 1** (dc1, dc2 into next st) 3 times (9)
**Rnds 2–3** dc (2 rnds)

**Rnd 4** (dc1, dc2tog) 3 times (6)
**Rnd 5** (dc1, dc2tog) twice (4)
Do not stuff.

## LEGS (make four)

Working in Charcoal
Begin by dc6 into ring
**Rnd 1** (dc2 into next st) 6 times (12)
Change to Cream and work 2cm LOOP STITCH (see page 93) every other stitch, getting longer up the leg
**Rnds 2–3** dc (2 rnds)
**Rnd 4** (dc1, dc2tog) 4 times (8)
**Rnds 5–8** dc (4 rnds)
Change to Chestnut and continue without loops
**Rnds 9–12** dc (4 rnds)
Stuff end and sew flat across top to close.

## TAIL

Working in Charcoal
Work ten 12cm KNOT LENGTHS (see page 101) on bottom.

## MANE

Working in Charcoal
Work ten 3cm KNOT LENGTHS (see page 101) between ears and down head.

## FACIAL MARKING

Using a sewing needle with two strands of Cream yarn held together, sew two large stitches across four rnds from muzzle upwards to create a flash.

Finish by sewing eyes into place with Black yarn.

**KNOTTING ON LENGTHS**

1 Insert the hook through the fabric around a stitch.

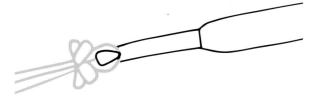

2 Yarn over with the middle of a length of yarn (or several held together) and pull through the stitch to form a loop.

3 Thread the ends of the yarn through the loop and pull to tighten to the fabric. Trim if necessary.

# HIGHLAND COW

COLOURS | CAMEL, OATMEAL

## BODY

Working in Camel

Work 1cm LOOP STITCH (see page 93) every third st on odd rnds and fifth st on even rnds

Begin by dc6 into ring

**Rnd 1** (dc2 into next st) 6 times (12 sts)
**Rnd 2** (dc1, dc2 into next st) 6 times (18)
**Rnd 3** (dc2, dc2 into next st) 6 times (24)
**Rnds 4–8** dc (5 rnds)
**Rnd 9** dc9, (dc2tog) 3 times, dc9 (21)
**Rnd 10** (dc5, dc2tog) 3 times (18)
**Rnds 11–13** dc (3 rnds)
**Rnd 14** (dc4, dc2tog) 3 times (15)
**Rnd 15** (dc3, dc2tog) 3 times (12)
**Rnd 16** (dc2tog) 6 times (6)

## HEAD

Working in Camel

Work 1cm LOOP STITCH (see page 93) every second st on odd rnds and third st on even rnds

Begin by dc6 into ring

**Rnd 1** (dc2 into next st) 6 times (12)
**Rnd 2** (dc1, dc2 into next st) 6 times (18)
**Rnd 3** (dc2, dc2 into next st) 6 times (24)
**Rnds 4–6** dc (3 rnds)
Change to Oatmeal and continue without loops
**Rnds 7–8** sc (2 rnds)

## LEGS (make four)

Working in Camel

Work 1cm LOOP STITCH (see page 93) every third st on odd rnds and fifth st on even rnds

Begin by dc6 into ring

**Rnd 1** (dc2 into next st) 6 times (12)
**Rnds 2–3** dc (2 rnds)
**Rnd 4** (dc1, dc2tog) 4 times (8)
**Rnds 5–12** dc (8 rnds)
Stuff end and sew flat across top to close.

## EARS (make two)

Working in Camel

Work 1cm LOOP STITCH (see page 93) every other st throughout

Begin by dc5 into ring

**Rnd 1** dc
Do not stuff.

## HORNS (make two)

Working in Oatmeal

Ch6 and sl st to join into a circle

**Rnds 1–2** dc (2 rnds)
**Rnd 3** dc2tog, dc4 (5)
**Rnds 4–5** dc (2 rnds)
**Rnd 6** dc2tog, dc3 (4)
**Rnd 7** (dc2tog) twice (2)

## TAIL

Working in Camel

Create CHAIN TAIL (see page 55): sl st into tail position, then work three ch6 CHAIN LOOPS (see page 33) onto end.

Finish by sewing eyes and nostrils into place with Black yarn.

# OTHERS IN THE SERIES

These mini Edward's Menagerie animal patterns are part of a wider collection of more minis and larger animal crochet patterns. In the whole range there are now over five hundred different animal patterns.

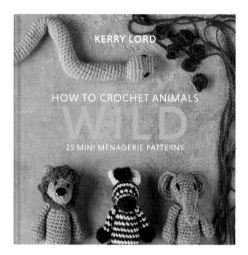

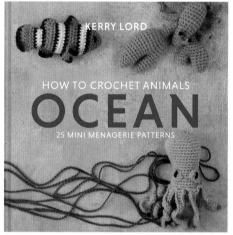

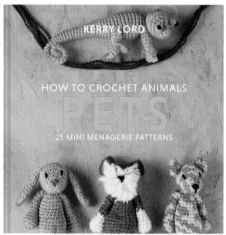

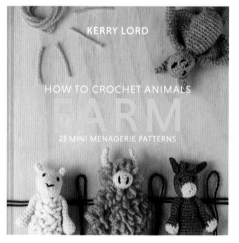

This cat pattern can be found in
*How to Crochet Animals: PETS*

# BE SOCIAL

One of the most exciting things about crocheting is joining the active online community helping and inspiring each every day in their shared hobby. Share your makes using the tag #edsanimals to join in.

**ON THIS PAGE**

@shazam75
@mcginnis.marg
@janawill73

**ON THE OPPOSITE PAGE**

@jamesmakesthings
@vanholsti
@vickirichardsgreen
@jo.lovingcrochet
@twistedlittlestitch77
@izzysdoodles
@pea_green_boat
@zenondebrujas
@hobbit_gen

# ANIMAL INDEX

| | | | | |
|---|---|---|---|---|
| **ALPACA** | 34 | | **HEDGEHOG** | 36 |
| **BADGER** | 62 | | **HIGHLAND COW** | 102 |
| **BAT** | 80 | | **MOLE** | 64 |
| **BORDER COLLIE** | 96 | | **PHEASANT** | 78 |
| **CHICK** | 48 | | **PIG** | 20 |
| **DONKEY** | 52 | | **PONY** | 60 |
| **DORSET DOWN SHEEP** | 68 | | **ROBIN** | 72 |
| **FOX** | 70 | | **SHEEP** | 30 |
| **FRIESIAN COW** | 76 | | **SHIRE HORSE** | 98 |
| **FROG** | 44 | | **SNAIL** | 88 |
| **GOAT** | 58 | | **SQUIRREL** | 94 |
| **GOOSE** | 40 | | **SWALEDALE SHEEP** | 84 |
| **HARE** | 28 | | | |

# TECHNIQUE INDEX

Please note, British English crochet terms are used throughout. Please see page 6 for more information.

Abbreviations *see* Reading a pattern
Adding the tail **26**

Back loops only, working into **87**

Chain (ch) **14**
  Chain loops **33**
  Chain tail **55**
  Chain, then slip stitch to join into
    a circle **43**

Changing colour **56**
Counting
  Counting a chain **17**
  Counting the stitches in a round **17**

DC6 into ring (magic circle) **15**
Decreasing (dc2tog) **16**
Double crochet stitch (dc) **15**

Eyes/nostrils, sewing on **26**

Fastening off **16**
Finishing
  Eyes/nostrils, sewing on **26**
  Fastening off **16**
  Gathering stitches **24**
  Order of sewing **23**
  Oversewing a leg **24**

Gathering stitches **24**

Half treble crochet stitch (htr) **75**
Hand positions
  Holding your hook **12**
  Holding your yarn **13**

Knotting on lengths **101**

Loop stitch **93**

Magic circle *see* DC6 into ring

Order of sewing **23**
Oversewing a leg **24**

Reading a pattern and
  abbreviations **18**

Sewing on eyes/nostrils **26**
Sewing on a piece **87**
Sewing together **91**
Slip knot **14**
Slip stitch
  Slip stitch chains **39**
  Slip stitch traverse **39**
Spiral crochet **19**
Splitting the round **51**
Stuffing **23**

Treble crochet stitch (tr) **75**

Working wings **83**

# THANKS

The exciting style in this book has only been made possible with the talented pen of Evelyn Birch, who has patiently captured my hands and hook in illustrations that will make it even easier to learn to crochet. Her assistance in the creation of this mini Edward's Menagerie series has sparked a new direction and I have thoroughly enjoyed collaborating to create such beautiful books.

Special thanks to Evelyn Birch and Rachel Critchley for quite a few rainy Summer days fueled by custard tarts spent hooking up spare legs, endless snakes and testing patterns.

A specific thank you to TOFT team members Jo Clements, Nathasja Vermaning and Helen Wyatt for their extra neat stitches and speedy hooks which help make the lovely photography in this book possible. Wider thanks are due to the TOFT team (past and present) who work hard everyday to deliver TOFT products around the world, and help our customers learn to crochet and enjoy the craft as much as we do. Working alongside a group of such brilliant and enthusiastic people is an honor.

Without the support of my family I could not continue to run an expanding business, so a particular thanks goes to Doug Lord and my parents in continuing to enable me to follow my dreams.

Every year Edward gets closer to gaining the coordination and concentration to be able to make his own first crochet animal. Perhaps one of these minis will be the one! My two children continue to inspire me with their constant feedback on what's flying off the end of my hook.

A final thanks to all the Edward's Menagerie fans out there who continue to support TOFT. Your passion for my designs and our yarns keeps me crocheting as fast as I can!